MY STORY

SET IN SOUL

THIS JOURNAL BELONGS TO

_____

DEDICATED TO EVERY
KID GROWING FORWARD
AND MOVING INTO THEIR
BRIGHTEST FUTURE.

TABLE OF CONTENTS

HOW TO USE THIS JOURNAL

So much is changing. In fact, so much has changed. It can be a lot to take in. Will things work out? What happens next? So many questions. The truth is, there is so much we carry along with us that may or may not be helping us. There are so many things that we may not understand. You now have a new family. Your new family is already in love with you and want to get to know you better but everything takes time. Learning to trust, let go, open up and feel comfortable are all things that take time but need to be done. This is how great relationships are formed. It's normal to have questions, thoughts and feelings you may not feel like anyone understands. This journal is your safe place to communicate those thoughts and feelings. The goal of this journal is to serve as your best friend. It is a place where you can truly confide in yourself as well as keep track of your growth during this time in your life without feeling misunderstood or judged. This is you loving on you. This is the place where you can write down or draw what you don't understand, why you feel that things are happening the way they are, what you want, what you look forward to and so on.

We want you to use this journal every night to reflect on your day. As you begin to fill out each daily journal prompt, you will start to feel a change within yourself. You will start to noticed how and why your thoughts are formed and how you are handling conflict and resolving issues. You are very special and your thoughts and feelings matter. You are not any different from any other kid. You have the brightest future ahead of you. Everything matters with what you do today and this journal will help you to move forward and grow with your new family as well as be your best self. This journal was designed for you to know you are not alone in your feelings. You are growing stronger and are surrounded with those who are already in love with you for who you are. You deserve the best. The motivational quotes within this journal are there to remind you of how great you are. Feel free to write down whatever comes to mind in the freestyling sections. The only thing required from you is an open heart, honesty and consistency. So let's get started.

WHAT I KNOW

WHAT I KNOW

I Was Adopted At The Age Of:

My Birthday Is:

I Was Born (Write Down Where):

My Adoptive Parents Are:

My Biological Parent's Names:

A DEEPER
UNDERSTANDING
OF ME

A DEEPER UNDERSTANDING OF ME

What I Like To Do:

I Like To Eat:

I Am Good At:

Do I Have Sibilings?

I Want To Become:

A DEEPER UNDERSTANDING OF ME

I Am Grateful For:

My Favorite Number:

I Currently Feel:

It's Going To Take Time For Me To:

I Wish I Knew How To:

A DEEPER UNDERSTANDING OF ME

I Get Nervous About:

My Favorite Show:

I Like To Think About:

I Try My Best To:

What I Love About Myself:

A DEEPER UNDERSTANDING OF ME

I Believe:

I Look Forward To:

My Favorite Song Right Now:

I Want To:

It Feels Good Knowing:

A DEEPER UNDERSTANDING OF ME

It's Hard For Me To Believe:

I Love:

I Need Help With:

I Want To Know The Truth About:

I'm Afraid That:

A DEEPER UNDERSTANDING OF ME

I Dream Of:

I Feel Safe When:

When I Grow Up, I Want To:

I Want To Be Known For:

What I Do Like:

A DEEPER UNDERSTANDING OF ME

What I Don't Like:

I Feel Like I Need:

I Just Want:

What I Would Like To Do Differently:

I Am Getting Better At Doing:

A DEEPER UNDERSTANDING OF ME

I Love That I Am:

I Know That I Am:

I Feel Great Knowing:

I Am Preparing For My Future By:

I Now View Things:

A DEEPER UNDERSTANDING OF ME

I Changed My Mind About:

When I Don't Get My Way, I:

I Am Special Because:

What I Love About Me:

I Did Good At:

18

A DEEPER UNDERSTANDING OF ME

I Don't Know How To Handle:

A Healthy Friendship To Me Is:

I Want A Friend Who:

I Know I Don't Need:

The Reason Why I _____ Is

Because _____.

A DEEPER UNDERSTANDING OF ME

I'm Interested In:

I Want To Feel:

I Think I Am:

I Want To Get Better At:

I Know I Can:

A DEEPER UNDERSTANDING OF ME

I Know I Am Loveable Because:

When My Feelings Are Hurt, I:

I Get Excited About:

What Makes Me Smile?

I Know I Am Important Because:

A DEEPER UNDERSTANDING OF ME

I Can't Wait Until:

I Want To Tell Someone I Trust That:

Who Do I Trust?

What Currently Bothers Me?

My Favorite Animal:

A DEEPER UNDERSTANDING OF ME

The Most Precious Thing I Own:

When I Get Older, I Want:

I Remember:

The Day I Found Out I Was Adopted, I:

Why Do I Think My Adoptive Parents Chose Me?

A DEEPER UNDERSTANDING OF ME

What Do I Know Happened To My Biological Parents?

Do I Feel Like I Get Treated Like My Adoptive Parent's Biological Kids? (Answer If Applicable)?

I Feel Like I Get Treated:

I Want To Be The Best:

I Don't Feel Accepted Being:

A DEEPER UNDERSTANDING OF ME

I Feel Like I Can Be:

I Feel Like Things Are:

I Want To Go To:

I Have Learned:

I Have Confidence In:

A DEEPER UNDERSTANDING OF ME

I Don't Like Talking About:

Why To The Above Prompt?

I Forgive:

I Know I Am Not The Reason For:

I Use To Blame Myself For:

A DEEPER UNDERSTANDING OF ME

I Am Growing Confident In Myself By:

Positive Things About Me:

Everyday Is A New Day To:

Family Means To Me:

My Ideal Family:

A DEEPER UNDERSTANDING OF ME

My Ideal Sense Of Family Is:

My Adoptive Parents Told Me:

I Think My Adoptive Parents Are:

I Feel Comfortable:

When I See Other Kids With Their Families, I:

A DEEPER UNDERSTANDING OF ME

What I Know About My Birth Parents:

OPENING MYSELF UP TO GREATNESS

OPENING MYSELF UP TO GREATNESS

Date: Mood:

Today I Felt: Today I Wanted To Know:

Today I Was Able To: Today I Am Thankful For:

Today I Enjoyed: What Bothered Me Today?

Today I Thought About: I Am Getting Better At:

Why To The Answer I Gave To The   I Am Starting To Feel _____
Prompt Above?

I Think Life Is: About _____.

OPENING MYSELF UP TO GREATNESS

Date: Mood:

Today I Felt: Today I Wanted To Know:

Today I Was Able To: Today I Am Thankful For:

Today I Enjoyed: What Bothered Me Today?

Today I Thought About: I Am Getting Better At:

Why To The Answer I Gave To The   I Am Starting To Feel _____
Prompt Above?

I Think Life Is: About _____.

TODAY IS THE START OF MY NEW LIFE.

OPENING MYSELF UP TO GREATNESS

Date: Mood:

Today I Felt: Today I Wanted To Know:

Today I Was Able To: Today I Am Thankful For:

Today I Enjoyed: What Bothered Me Today?

Today I Thought About: I Am Getting Better At:

Why To The Answer I Gave To The   I Am Starting To Feel _____
Prompt Above?

I Think Life Is: About _____.

OPENING MYSELF UP TO GREATNESS

Date: Mood:

Today I Felt: Today I Wanted To Know:

Today I Was Able To: Today I Am Thankful For:

Today I Enjoyed: What Bothered Me Today?

Today I Thought About: I Am Getting Better At:

Why To The Answer I Gave To The   I Am Starting To Feel _____
Prompt Above?

I Think Life Is: About _____.

7 THINGS THAT MAKE ME SPECIAL....

1.

2.

3.

4.

5.

6.

7.

GOD IS WITH ME EVERY STEP OF THE WAY.

OPENING MYSELF UP TO GREATNESS

Date: Mood:

Today I Felt: Today I Wanted To Know:

Today I Was Able To: Today I Am Thankful For:

Today I Enjoyed: What Bothered Me Today?

Today I Thought About: I Am Getting Better At:

Why To The Answer I Gave To The   I Am Starting To Feel _____
Prompt Above?

I Think Life Is: About _____.

OPENING MYSELF UP TO GREATNESS

Date: Mood:

Today I Felt: Today I Wanted To Know:

Today I Was Able To: Today I Am Thankful For:

Today I Enjoyed: What Bothered Me Today?

Today I Thought About: I Am Getting Better At:

Why To The Answer I Gave To The   I Am Starting To Feel _____
Prompt Above?

I Think Life Is: About _____.

OPENING MYSELF UP TO GREATNESS

Date: Mood:

Today I Felt: Today I Wanted To Know:

Today I Was Able To: Today I Am Thankful For:

Today I Enjoyed: What Bothered Me Today?

Today I Thought About: I Am Getting Better At:

Why To The Answer I Gave To The   I Am Starting To Feel _____
Prompt Above?

I Think Life Is: About _____.

MY FUTURE IS TOO BRIGHT TO LOOK BACK.

FROM THIS POINT ON, EVERYTHING WILL BE ALRIGHT.

OPENING MYSELF UP TO GREATNESS

Date: Mood:

Today I Felt: Today I Wanted To Know:

Today I Was Able To: Today I Am Thankful For:

Today I Enjoyed: What Bothered Me Today?

Today I Thought About: I Am Getting Better At:

Why To The Answer I Gave To The   I Am Starting To Feel _____
Prompt Above?

I Think Life Is: About _____.

OPENING MYSELF UP TO GREATNESS

Date: Mood:

Today I Felt: Today I Wanted To Know:

Today I Was Able To: Today I Am Thankful For:

Today I Enjoyed: What Bothered Me Today?

Today I Thought About: I Am Getting Better At:

Why To The Answer I Gave To The   I Am Starting To Feel _____
Prompt Above?

I Think Life Is: About _____.

OPENING MYSELF UP TO GREATNESS

Date: Mood:

Today I Felt: Today I Wanted To Know:

Today I Was Able To: Today I Am Thankful For:

Today I Enjoyed: What Bothered Me Today?

Today I Thought About: I Am Getting Better At:

Why To The Answer I Gave To The   I Am Starting To Feel _____
Prompt Above?

I Think Life Is: About _____.

MY THOUGHTS AND/OR MY DRAWINGS

OPENING MYSELF UP TO GREATNESS

Date: Mood:

Today I Felt: Today I Wanted To Know:

Today I Was Able To: Today I Am Thankful For:

Today I Enjoyed: What Bothered Me Today?

Today I Thought About: I Am Getting Better At:

Why To The Answer I Gave To The   I Am Starting To Feel _____
Prompt Above?

I Think Life Is: About _____.

OPENING MYSELF UP TO GREATNESS

Date: Mood:

Today I Felt: | Today I Wanted To Know:

Today I Was Able To: | Today I Am Thankful For:

Today I Enjoyed: | What Bothered Me Today?

Today I Thought About: | I Am Getting Better At:

Why To The Answer I Gave To The | I Am Starting To Feel _____
Prompt Above?

I Think Life Is: | About _____.

OPENING MYSELF UP TO GREATNESS

Date: Mood:

Today I Felt: Today I Wanted To Know:

Today I Was Able To: Today I Am Thankful For:

Today I Enjoyed: What Bothered Me Today?

Today I Thought About: I Am Getting Better At:

Why To The Answer I Gave To The   I Am Starting To Feel _____
Prompt Above?

I Think Life Is: About _____.

I AM NOT THE ONLY ONE LOOKING OUT FOR MY BEST INTEREST.

SPOILER ALERT: I AM WINNING.

OPENING MYSELF UP TO GREATNESS

Date: Mood:

Today I Felt: Today I Wanted To Know:

Today I Was Able To: Today I Am Thankful For:

Today I Enjoyed: What Bothered Me Today?

Today I Thought About: I Am Getting Better At:

Why To The Answer I Gave To The   I Am Starting To Feel _____
Prompt Above?

I Think Life Is: About _____.

OPENING MYSELF UP TO GREATNESS

Date: Mood:

Today I Felt: Today I Wanted To Know:

Today I Was Able To: Today I Am Thankful For:

Today I Enjoyed: What Bothered Me Today?

Today I Thought About: I Am Getting Better At:

Why To The Answer I Gave To The   I Am Starting To Feel _____
Prompt Above?

I Think Life Is: About _____.

OPENING MYSELF UP TO GREATNESS

Date: Mood:

Today I Felt: Today I Wanted To Know:

Today I Was Able To: Today I Am Thankful For:

Today I Enjoyed: What Bothered Me Today?

Today I Thought About: I Am Getting Better At:

Why To The Answer I Gave To The   I Am Starting To Feel _____
Prompt Above?

I Think Life Is: About _____.

MY FAMILY IS PRETTY AWESOME.

IT'S OKAY TO BE DIFFERENT.

OPENING MYSELF UP TO GREATNESS

Date: Mood:

Today I Felt: Today I Wanted To Know:

Today I Was Able To: Today I Am Thankful For:

Today I Enjoyed: What Bothered Me Today?

Today I Thought About: I Am Getting Better At:

Why To The Answer I Gave To The   I Am Starting To Feel _____
Prompt Above?

I Think Life Is: About _____.

OPENING MYSELF UP TO GREATNESS

Date: Mood:

Today I Felt: Today I Wanted To Know:

Today I Was Able To: Today I Am Thankful For:

Today I Enjoyed: What Bothered Me Today?

Today I Thought About: I Am Getting Better At:

Why To The Answer I Gave To The   I Am Starting To Feel _____
Prompt Above?

I Think Life Is: About _____ .

OPENING MYSELF UP TO GREATNESS

Date: Mood:

Today I Felt: Today I Wanted To Know:

Today I Was Able To: Today I Am Thankful For:

Today I Enjoyed: What Bothered Me Today?

Today I Thought About: I Am Getting Better At:

Why To The Answer I Gave To The   I Am Starting To Feel _____
Prompt Above?

I Think Life Is: About _____.

MY THOUGHTS AND/OR MY DRAWINGS

OPENING MYSELF UP TO GREATNESS

Date: Mood:

Today I Felt: Today I Wanted To Know:

Today I Was Able To: Today I Am Thankful For:

Today I Enjoyed: What Bothered Me Today?

Today I Thought About: I Am Getting Better At:

Why To The Answer I Gave To The   I Am Starting To Feel _____
Prompt Above?

I Think Life Is: About _____.

OPENING MYSELF UP TO GREATNESS

Date: Mood:

Today I Felt: Today I Wanted To Know:

Today I Was Able To: Today I Am Thankful For:

Today I Enjoyed: What Bothered Me Today?

Today I Thought About: I Am Getting Better At:

Why To The Answer I Gave To The   I Am Starting To Feel _____
Prompt Above?

I Think Life Is: About _____.

OPENING MYSELF UP TO GREATNESS

Date: Mood:

Today I Felt: Today I Wanted To Know:

Today I Was Able To: Today I Am Thankful For:

Today I Enjoyed: What Bothered Me Today?

Today I Thought About: I Am Getting Better At:

Why To The Answer I Gave To The   I Am Starting To Feel _____
Prompt Above?

I Think Life Is: About _____.

MY THOUGHTS AND/OR MY DRAWINGS

OPENING MYSELF UP TO GREATNESS

Date: Mood:

Today I Felt: Today I Wanted To Know:

Today I Was Able To: Today I Am Thankful For:

Today I Enjoyed: What Bothered Me Today?

Today I Thought About: I Am Getting Better At:

Why To The Answer I Gave To The   I Am Starting To Feel _____
Prompt Above?

I Think Life Is: About _____.

OPENING MYSELF UP TO GREATNESS

Date: Mood:

Today I Felt·   Today I Wanted To Know:

Today I Was Able To: Today I Am Thankful For:

Today I Enjoyed: What Bothered Me Today?

Today I Thought About: I Am Getting Better At:

Why To The Answer I Gave To The   I Am Starting To Feel _____
Prompt Above?

I Think Life Is: About _____.

I AM CONFIDENT THAT I AM GOING TO GROW UP AND DO SO MANY WONDERFUL THINGS.

OPENING MYSELF UP TO GREATNESS

Date: Mood:

Today I Felt: Today I Wanted To Know:

Today I Was Able To: Today I Am Thankful For:

Today I Enjoyed: What Bothered Me Today?

Today I Thought About: I Am Getting Better At:

Why To The Answer I Gave To The   I Am Starting To Feel _____
Prompt Above?

I Think Life Is: About _____.

OPENING MYSELF UP TO GREATNESS

Date: Mood:

Today I Felt: Today I Wanted To Know:

Today I Was Able To: Today I Am Thankful For:

Today I Enjoyed: What Bothered Me Today?

Today I Thought About: I Am Getting Better At:

Why To The Answer I Gave To The   I Am Starting To Feel _____
Prompt Above?

I Think Life Is: About _____.

I KNOW I DESERVE....

MY THOUGHTS AND/OR MY DRAWINGS

OPENING MYSELF UP TO GREATNESS

Date: Mood:

Today I Felt: Today I Wanted To Know:

Today I Was Able To: Today I Am Thankful For:

Today I Enjoyed: What Bothered Me Today?

Today I Thought About: I Am Getting Better At:

Why To The Answer I Gave To The   I Am Starting To Feel _____
Prompt Above?

I Think Life Is: About _____.

OPENING MYSELF UP TO GREATNESS

Date: Mood:

Today I Felt: Today I Wanted To Know:

Today I Was Able To: Today I Am Thankful For:

Today I Enjoyed: What Bothered Me Today?

Today I Thought About: I Am Getting Better At:

Why To The Answer I Gave To The   I Am Starting To Feel _____
Prompt Above?

I Think Life Is: About _____.

OPENING MYSELF UP TO GREATNESS

Date: Mood:

Today I Felt: Today I Wanted To Know:

Today I Was Able To: Today I Am Thankful For:

Today I Enjoyed: What Bothered Me Today?

Today I Thought About: I Am Getting Better At:

Why To The Answer I Gave To The   I Am Starting To Feel _____
Prompt Above?

I Think Life Is: About _____.

OPENING MYSELF UP TO GREATNESS

Date: Mood:

Today I Felt: Today I Wanted To Know:

Today I Was Able To: Today I Am Thankful For:

Today I Enjoyed: What Bothered Me Today?

Today I Thought About: I Am Getting Better At:

Why To The Answer I Gave To The   I Am Starting To Feel _____
Prompt Above?

I Think Life Is: About _____.

EVERYTHING I'M LOOKING FOR IS WITHIN ME. THAT IS WHY I TREAT MYSELF GOOD. THAT IS WHY I SAY GOOD THINGS ABOUT MYSELF.

I KNOW MY
ADOPTIVE PARENTS ARE....

OPENING MYSELF UP TO GREATNESS

Date: Mood:

Today I Felt: Today I Wanted To Know:

Today I Was Able To: Today I Am Thankful For:

Today I Enjoyed: What Bothered Me Today?

Today I Thought About: I Am Getting Better At:

Why To The Answer I Gave To The   I Am Starting To Feel _____
Prompt Above?

I Think Life Is: About _____.

OPENING MYSELF UP TO GREATNESS

Date: Mood:

Today I Felt: Today I Wanted To Know:

Today I Was Able To: Today I Am Thankful For:

Today I Enjoyed: What Bothered Me Today?

Today I Thought About: I Am Getting Better At:

Why To The Answer I Gave To The   I Am Starting To Feel _____
Prompt Above?

I Think Life Is: About _____.

OPENING MYSELF UP TO GREATNESS

Date: Mood:

Today I Felt: Today I Wanted To Know:

Today I Was Able To: Today I Am Thankful For:

Today I Enjoyed: What Bothered Me Today?

Today I Thought About: I Am Getting Better At:

Why To The Answer I Gave To The   I Am Starting To Feel _____
Prompt Above?

I Think Life Is: About _____.

OPENING MYSELF UP TO GREATNESS

Date: Mood:

Today I Felt: Today I Wanted To Know:

Today I Was Able To: Today I Am Thankful For:

Today I Enjoyed: What Bothered Me Today?

Today I Thought About: I Am Getting Better At:

Why To The Answer I Gave To The   I Am Starting To Feel _____
Prompt Above?

I Think Life Is: About _____.

MY THOUGHTS AND/OR MY DRAWINGS

I AM WORTHY OF THE BEST.

I CONSIDER MYSELF BLESSED THAT GOD GAVE ME A PARENT THAT WILL BE WITH ME.

OPENING MYSELF UP TO GREATNESS

Date: Mood:

Today I Felt: Today I Wanted To Know:

Today I Was Able To: Today I Am Thankful For:

Today I Enjoyed: What Bothered Me Today?

Today I Thought About: I Am Getting Better At:

Why To The Answer I Gave To The   I Am Starting To Feel _____
Prompt Above?

I Think Life Is: About _____.

OPENING MYSELF UP TO GREATNESS

Date: Mood:

Today I Felt: Today I Wanted To Know:

Today I Was Able To: Today I Am Thankful For:

Today I Enjoyed: What Bothered Me Today?

Today I Thought About: I Am Getting Better At:

Why To The Answer I Gave To The   I Am Starting To Feel _____
Prompt Above?

I Think Life Is: About _____.

OPENING MYSELF UP TO GREATNESS

Date: Mood:

Today I Felt: Today I Wanted To Know:

Today I Was Able To: Today I Am Thankful For:

Today I Enjoyed: What Bothered Me Today?

Today I Thought About: I Am Getting Better At:

Why To The Answer I Gave To The   I Am Starting To Feel _____
Prompt Above?

I Think Life Is: About _____.

IN THE BEGINNING IT WAS HARD FOR ME TO....

OPENING MYSELF UP TO GREATNESS

Date: Mood:

Today I Felt: Today I Wanted To Know:

Today I Was Able To: Today I Am Thankful For:

Today I Enjoyed: What Bothered Me Today?

Today I Thought About: I Am Getting Better At:

Why To The Answer I Gave To The   I Am Starting To Feel _____
Prompt Above?

I Think Life Is: About _____.

OPENING MYSELF UP TO GREATNESS

Date: Mood:

Today I Felt:	Today I Wanted To Know:
Today I Was Able To:	Today I Am Thankful For:
Today I Enjoyed:	What Bothered Me Today?
Today I Thought About:	I Am Getting Better At:
Why To The Answer I Gave To The Prompt Above?	I Am Starting To Feel _____
I Think Life Is:	About _____.

90

OPENING MYSELF UP TO GREATNESS

Date: Mood:

Today I Felt: Today I Wanted To Know:

Today I Was Able To: Today I Am Thankful For:

Today I Enjoyed: What Bothered Me Today?

Today I Thought About: I Am Getting Better At:

Why To The Answer I Gave To The   I Am Starting To Feel _____
Prompt Above?

I Think Life Is: About _____.

I WITHDRAW WHEN....

OPENING MYSELF UP TO GREATNESS

Date: Mood:

Today I Felt: | Today I Wanted To Know:

Today I Was Able To: | Today I Am Thankful For:

Today I Enjoyed: | What Bothered Me Today?

Today I Thought About: | I Am Getting Better At:

Why To The Answer I Gave To The | I Am Starting To Feel _____
Prompt Above?

I Think Life Is: | About _____.

OPENING MYSELF UP TO GREATNESS

Date: Mood:

Today I Felt: Today I Wanted To Know:

Today I Was Able To: Today I Am Thankful For:

Today I Enjoyed: What Bothered Me Today?

Today I Thought About: I Am Getting Better At:

Why To The Answer I Gave To The   I Am Starting To Feel _____
Prompt Above?

I Think Life Is: About _____.

I AM GETTING BETTER AT ....

OPENING MYSELF UP TO GREATNESS

Date: Mood:

Today I Felt: Today I Wanted To Know:

Today I Was Able To: Today I Am Thankful For:

Today I Enjoyed: What Bothered Me Today?

Today I Thought About: I Am Getting Better At:

Why To The Answer I Gave To The   I Am Starting To Feel _____
Prompt Above?

I Think Life Is: About _____.

96

OPENING MYSELF UP TO GREATNESS

Date: Mood:

Today I Felt: Today I Wanted To Know:

Today I Was Able To: Today I Am Thankful For:

Today I Enjoyed: What Bothered Me Today?

Today I Thought About: I Am Getting Better At:

Why To The Answer I Gave To The   I Am Starting To Feel _____
Prompt Above?

I Think Life Is: About _____.

OPENING MYSELF UP TO GREATNESS

Date: Mood:

Today I Felt: Today I Wanted To Know:

Today I Was Able To: Today I Am Thankful For:

Today I Enjoyed: What Bothered Me Today?

Today I Thought About: I Am Getting Better At:

Why To The Answer I Gave To The   I Am Starting To Feel _____
Prompt Above?

I Think Life Is: About _____.

I AM AT PEACE WITH EVERYTHING THAT HAS HAPPENED.

I HAVE SO MUCH TO LOOK FORWARD TO.

OPENING MYSELF UP TO GREATNESS

Date: Mood:

Today I Felt: Today I Wanted To Know:

Today I Was Able To: Today I Am Thankful For:

Today I Enjoyed: What Bothered Me Today?

Today I Thought About: I Am Getting Better At:

Why To The Answer I Gave To The   I Am Starting To Feel _____
Prompt Above?

I Think Life Is: About _____.

OPENING MYSELF UP TO GREATNESS

Date: Mood:

Today I Felt: Today I Wanted To Know:

Today I Was Able To: Today I Am Thankful For:

Today I Enjoyed: What Bothered Me Today?

Today I Thought About: I Am Getting Better At:

Why To The Answer I Gave To The   I Am Starting To Feel _____
Prompt Above?

I Think Life Is: About _____.

OPENING MYSELF UP TO GREATNESS

Date: Mood:

Today I Felt: Today I Wanted To Know:

Today I Was Able To: Today I Am Thankful For:

Today I Enjoyed: What Bothered Me Today?

Today I Thought About: I Am Getting Better At:

Why To The Answer I Gave To The   I Am Starting To Feel _____
Prompt Above?

I Think Life Is: About _____.

I AM PRETTY AMAZING AT....

MY THOUGHTS AND/OR MY DRAWINGS

OPENING MYSELF UP TO GREATNESS

Date: Mood:

Today I Felt: Today I Wanted To Know:

Today I Was Able To: Today I Am Thankful For:

Today I Enjoyed: What Bothered Me Today?

Today I Thought About: I Am Getting Better At:

Why To The Answer I Gave To The   I Am Starting To Feel _____
Prompt Above?

I Think Life Is: About _____.

OPENING MYSELF UP TO GREATNESS

Date: Mood:

Today I Felt: Today I Wanted To Know:

Today I Was Able To: Today I Am Thankful For:

Today I Enjoyed: What Bothered Me Today?

Today I Thought About: I Am Getting Better At:

Why To The Answer I Gave To The   I Am Starting To Feel _____
Prompt Above?

I Think Life Is: About _____.

OPENING MYSELF UP TO GREATNESS

Date: Mood:

Today I Felt: Today I Wanted To Know:

Today I Was Able To: Today I Am Thankful For:

Today I Enjoyed: What Bothered Me Today?

Today I Thought About: I Am Getting Better At:

Why To The Answer I Gave To The   I Am Starting To Feel _____
Prompt Above?

I Think Life Is: About _____.

I LOVE WHO I AM.

OPENING MYSELF UP TO GREATNESS

Date: Mood:

Today I Felt: Today I Wanted To Know:

Today I Was Able To: Today I Am Thankful For:

Today I Enjoyed: What Bothered Me Today?

Today I Thought About: I Am Getting Better At:

Why To The Answer I Gave To The   I Am Starting To Feel _____
Prompt Above?

I Think Life Is: About _____ .

OPENING MYSELF UP TO GREATNESS

Date: Mood:

Today I Felt: Today I Wanted To Know:

Today I Was Able To: Today I Am Thankful For:

Today I Enjoyed: What Bothered Me Today?

Today I Thought About: I Am Getting Better At:

Why To The Answer I Gave To The   I Am Starting To Feel _____
Prompt Above?

I Think Life Is: About _____.

MY THOUGHTS AND/OR MY DRAWINGS

WHAT DO I FEEL IS HOLDING ME BACK?

OPENING MYSELF UP TO GREATNESS

Date: Mood:

Today I Felt: Today I Wanted To Know:

Today I Was Able To: Today I Am Thankful For:

Today I Enjoyed: What Bothered Me Today?

Today I Thought About: I Am Getting Better At:

Why To The Answer I Gave To The   I Am Starting To Feel _____
Prompt Above?

I Think Life Is: About _____.

OPENING MYSELF UP TO GREATNESS

Date: Mood:

Today I Felt: Today I Wanted To Know:

Today I Was Able To: Today I Am Thankful For:

Today I Enjoyed: What Bothered Me Today?

Today I Thought About: I Am Getting Better At:

Why To The Answer I Gave To The   I Am Starting To Feel _____
Prompt Above?

I Think Life Is: About _____.

OPENING MYSELF UP TO GREATNESS

Date: Mood:

Today I Felt: Today I Wanted To Know:

Today I Was Able To: Today I Am Thankful For:

Today I Enjoyed: What Bothered Me Today?

Today I Thought About: I Am Getting Better At:

Why To The Answer I Gave To The   I Am Starting To Feel _____
Prompt Above?

I Think Life Is: About _____ .

I WON'T LET MY PAST BLOCK MY FUTURE BLESSINGS.

EVERYDAY I FEEL MORE AND MORE LIKE MYSELF.

OPENING MYSELF UP TO GREATNESS

Date: Mood:

Today I Felt: Today I Wanted To Know:

Today I Was Able To: Today I Am Thankful For:

Today I Enjoyed: What Bothered Me Today?

Today I Thought About: I Am Getting Better At:

Why To The Answer I Gave To The   I Am Starting To Feel _____
Prompt Above?

I Think Life Is: About _____.

OPENING MYSELF UP TO GREATNESS

Date: Mood:

Today I Felt: Today I Wanted To Know:

Today I Was Able To: Today I Am Thankful For:

Today I Enjoyed: What Bothered Me Today?

Today I Thought About: I Am Getting Better At:

Why To The Answer I Gave To The   I Am Starting To Feel _____
Prompt Above?

I Think Life Is: About _____.

OPENING MYSELF UP TO GREATNESS

Date: Mood:

Today I Felt: Today I Wanted To Know:

Today I Was Able To: Today I Am Thankful For:

Today I Enjoyed: What Bothered Me Today?

Today I Thought About: I Am Getting Better At:

Why To The Answer I Gave To The   I Am Starting To Feel _____
Prompt Above?

I Think Life Is: About _____.

OPENING MYSELF UP TO GREATNESS

Date: Mood:

Today I Felt: Today I Wanted To Know:

Today I Was Able To: Today I Am Thankful For:

Today I Enjoyed: What Bothered Me Today?

Today I Thought About: I Am Getting Better At:

Why To The Answer I Gave To The   I Am Starting To Feel _____
Prompt Above?

I Think Life Is: About _____.

OPENING MYSELF UP TO GREATNESS

Date: Mood:

Today I Felt: Today I Wanted To Know:

Today I Was Able To: Today I Am Thankful For:

Today I Enjoyed: What Bothered Me Today?

Today I Thought About: I Am Getting Better At:

Why To The Answer I Gave To The   I Am Starting To Feel _____
Prompt Above?

I Think Life Is: About _____.

ONE DAY I HOPE TO....

MY THOUGHTS AND/OR MY DRAWINGS

OPENING MYSELF UP TO GREATNESS

Date: Mood:

Today I Felt: Today I Wanted To Know:

Today I Was Able To: Today I Am Thankful For:

Today I Enjoyed: What Bothered Me Today?

Today I Thought About: I Am Getting Better At:

Why To The Answer I Gave To The   I Am Starting To Feel _____
Prompt Above?

I Think Life Is: About _____.

OPENING MYSELF UP TO GREATNESS

Date: Mood:

Today I Felt: Today I Wanted To Know:

Today I Was Able To: Today I Am Thankful For:

Today I Enjoyed: What Bothered Me Today?

Today I Thought About: I Am Getting Better At:

Why To The Answer I Gave To The   I Am Starting To Feel _____
Prompt Above?

I Think Life Is: About _____.

OPENING MYSELF UP TO GREATNESS

Date: Mood:

Today I Felt: Today I Wanted To Know:

Today I Was Able To: Today I Am Thankful For:

Today I Enjoyed: What Bothered Me Today?

Today I Thought About: I Am Getting Better At:

Why To The Answer I Gave To The   I Am Starting To Feel _____
Prompt Above?

I Think Life Is: About _____.

EVERYONE MAKES MISTAKES BUT IT'S MY JOB TO DO BETTER.

MY JOURNEY IS BUILDING ME UP TOWARDS GREATNESS.

OPENING MYSELF UP TO GREATNESS

Date: Mood:

Today I Felt: Today I Wanted To Know:

Today I Was Able To: Today I Am Thankful For:

Today I Enjoyed: What Bothered Me Today?

Today I Thought About: I Am Getting Better At:

Why To The Answer I Gave To The   I Am Starting To Feel _____
Prompt Above?

I Think Life Is: About _____ .

OPENING MYSELF UP TO GREATNESS

Date: Mood:

Today I Felt: Today I Wanted To Know:

Today I Was Able To: Today I Am Thankful For:

Today I Enjoyed: What Bothered Me Today?

Today I Thought About: I Am Getting Better At:

Why To The Answer I Gave To The   I Am Starting To Feel _____
Prompt Above?

I Think Life Is: About _____.

OPENING MYSELF UP TO GREATNESS

Date: Mood:

Today I Felt: Today I Wanted To Know:

Today I Was Able To: Today I Am Thankful For:

Today I Enjoyed: What Bothered Me Today?

Today I Thought About: I Am Getting Better At:

Why To The Answer I Gave To The   I Am Starting To Feel _____
Prompt Above?

I Think Life Is: About _____.

I AM INTERESTED IN....

OPENING MYSELF UP TO GREATNESS

Date: Mood:

Today I Felt: Today I Wanted To Know:

Today I Was Able To: Today I Am Thankful For:

Today I Enjoyed: What Bothered Me Today?

Today I Thought About: I Am Getting Better At:

Why To The Answer I Gave To The   I Am Starting To Feel _____
Prompt Above?

I Think Life Is: About _____.

OPENING MYSELF UP TO GREATNESS

Date: Mood:

Today I Felt: Today I Wanted To Know:

Today I Was Able To: Today I Am Thankful For:

Today I Enjoyed: What Bothered Me Today?

Today I Thought About: I Am Getting Better At:

Why To The Answer I Gave To The   I Am Starting To Feel _____
Prompt Above?

I Think Life Is: About _____.

OPENING MYSELF UP TO GREATNESS

Date: Mood:

Today I Felt: Today I Wanted To Know:

Today I Was Able To: Today I Am Thankful For:

Today I Enjoyed: What Bothered Me Today?

Today I Thought About: I Am Getting Better At:

Why To The Answer I Gave To The   I Am Starting To Feel _____
Prompt Above?

I Think Life Is: About _____.

I HAVE ALWAYS BELIEVED....

THOUGH MY FATHER AND MOTHER FORSAKE ME, THE LORD WILL RECEIVE ME.

- PSALM 27:10

OPENING MYSELF UP TO GREATNESS

Date: Mood:

Today I Felt: Today I Wanted To Know:

Today I Was Able To: Today I Am Thankful For:

Today I Enjoyed: What Bothered Me Today?

Today I Thought About: I Am Getting Better At:

Why To The Answer I Gave To The   I Am Starting To Feel _____
Prompt Above?

I Think Life Is: About _____ .

OPENING MYSELF UP TO GREATNESS

Date: Mood:

Today I Felt: Today I Wanted To Know:

Today I Was Able To: Today I Am Thankful For:

Today I Enjoyed: What Bothered Me Today?

Today I Thought About: I Am Getting Better At:

Why To The Answer I Gave To The   I Am Starting To Feel _____
Prompt Above?

I Think Life Is: About _____.

OPENING MYSELF UP TO GREATNESS

Date: Mood:

Today I Felt: Today I Wanted To Know:

Today I Was Able To: Today I Am Thankful For:

Today I Enjoyed: What Bothered Me Today?

Today I Thought About: I Am Getting Better At:

Why To The Answer I Gave To The   I Am Starting To Feel _____
Prompt Above?

I Think Life Is: About _____.

TODAY I WILL LEARN TO FORGIVE.

EVERYTHING HAPPENS FOR A REASON.

OPENING MYSELF UP TO GREATNESS

Date: Mood:

Today I Felt: Today I Wanted To Know:

Today I Was Able To: Today I Am Thankful For:

Today I Enjoyed: What Bothered Me Today?

Today I Thought About: I Am Getting Better At:

Why To The Answer I Gave To The   I Am Starting To Feel _____
Prompt Above?

I Think Life Is: About _____.

OPENING MYSELF UP TO GREATNESS

Date: Mood:

Today I Felt: Today I Wanted To Know:

Today I Was Able To: Today I Am Thankful For:

Today I Enjoyed: What Bothered Me Today?

Today I Thought About: I Am Getting Better At:

Why To The Answer I Gave To The   I Am Starting To Feel _____
Prompt Above?

I Think Life Is: About _____.

MY THOUGHTS AND/OR MY DRAWINGS

OPENING MYSELF UP TO GREATNESS

Date: Mood:

Today I Felt: Today I Wanted To Know:

Today I Was Able To: Today I Am Thankful For:

Today I Enjoyed: What Bothered Me Today?

Today I Thought About: I Am Getting Better At:

Why To The Answer I Gave To The   I Am Starting To Feel _____
Prompt Above?

I Think Life Is: About _____.

OPENING MYSELF UP TO GREATNESS

Date: Mood:

Today I Felt: Today I Wanted To Know:

Today I Was Able To: Today I Am Thankful For:

Today I Enjoyed: What Bothered Me Today?

Today I Thought About: I Am Getting Better At:

Why To The Answer I Gave To The   I Am Starting To Feel _____
Prompt Above?

I Think Life Is: About _____.

I DREAM ABOUT....

LEARNING TO LOVE MY NEW PARENTS.

OPENING MYSELF UP TO GREATNESS

Date: Mood:

Today I Felt: Today I Wanted To Know:

Today I Was Able To: Today I Am Thankful For:

Today I Enjoyed: What Bothered Me Today?

Today I Thought About: I Am Getting Better At:

Why To The Answer I Gave To The   I Am Starting To Feel _____
Prompt Above?

I Think Life Is: About _____.

OPENING MYSELF UP TO GREATNESS

Date: Mood:

Today I Felt: Today I Wanted To Know:

Today I Was Able To: Today I Am Thankful For:

Today I Enjoyed: What Bothered Me Today?

Today I Thought About: I Am Getting Better At:

Why To The Answer I Gave To The   I Am Starting To Feel _____
Prompt Above?

I Think Life Is: About _____.

OPENING MYSELF UP TO GREATNESS

Date: Mood:

Today I Felt: Today I Wanted To Know:

Today I Was Able To: Today I Am Thankful For:

Today I Enjoyed: What Bothered Me Today?

Today I Thought About: I Am Getting Better At:

Why To The Answer I Gave To The   I Am Starting To Feel _____
Prompt Above?

I Think Life Is: About _____.

MY THOUGHTS AND/OR MY DRAWINGS

OPENING MYSELF UP TO GREATNESS

Date: Mood:

Today I Felt: Today I Wanted To Know:

Today I Was Able To: Today I Am Thankful For:

Today I Enjoyed: What Bothered Me Today?

Today I Thought About: I Am Getting Better At:

Why To The Answer I Gave To The   I Am Starting To Feel _____
Prompt Above?

I Think Life Is: About _____.

OPENING MYSELF UP TO GREATNESS

Date: Mood:

Today I Felt: Today I Wanted To Know:

Today I Was Able To: Today I Am Thankful For:

Today I Enjoyed: What Bothered Me Today?

Today I Thought About: I Am Getting Better At:

Why To The Answer I Gave To The   I Am Starting To Feel _____
Prompt Above?

I Think Life Is: About _____.

FIVE THINGS I WANT TO DO....

1.

2.

3.

4.

5.

I AM SIMPLY A CHILD, NOT AN ADOPTIVE CHILD.

OPENING MYSELF UP TO GREATNESS

Date: Mood:

Today I Felt: Today I Wanted To Know:

Today I Was Able To: Today I Am Thankful For:

Today I Enjoyed: What Bothered Me Today?

Today I Thought About: I Am Getting Better At:

Why To The Answer I Gave To The   I Am Starting To Feel _____
Prompt Above?

I Think Life Is: About _____ .

OPENING MYSELF UP TO GREATNESS

Date: Mood:

Today I Felt: Today I Wanted To Know:

Today I Was Able To: Today I Am Thankful For:

Today I Enjoyed: What Bothered Me Today?

Today I Thought About: I Am Getting Better At:

Why To The Answer I Gave To The   I Am Starting To Feel _____
Prompt Above?

I Think Life Is: About _____.

OPENING MYSELF UP TO GREATNESS

Date: Mood:

Today I Felt: Today I Wanted To Know:

Today I Was Able To: Today I Am Thankful For:

Today I Enjoyed: What Bothered Me Today?

Today I Thought About: I Am Getting Better At:

Why To The Answer I Gave To The   I Am Starting To Feel _____
Prompt Above?

I Think Life Is: About _____.

ONLY A FEW COULD AND WILL UNDERSTAND YOUR JOURNEY.

I CAN NOW LET GO OF ALL FEELINGS OF HURT.

OPENING MYSELF UP TO GREATNESS

Date: Mood:

Today I Felt: Today I Wanted To Know:

Today I Was Able To: Today I Am Thankful For:

Today I Enjoyed: What Bothered Me Today?

Today I Thought About: I Am Getting Better At:

Why To The Answer I Gave To The   I Am Starting To Feel _____
Prompt Above?

I Think Life Is: About _____.

OPENING MYSELF UP TO GREATNESS

Date: Mood:

Today I Felt: Today I Wanted To Know:

Today I Was Able To: Today I Am Thankful For:

Today I Enjoyed: What Bothered Me Today?

Today I Thought About: I Am Getting Better At:

Why To The Answer I Gave To The   I Am Starting To Feel _____
Prompt Above?

I Think Life Is: About _____.

OPENING MYSELF UP TO GREATNESS

Date: Mood:

Today I Felt: Today I Wanted To Know:

Today I Was Able To: Today I Am Thankful For:

Today I Enjoyed: What Bothered Me Today?

Today I Thought About: I Am Getting Better At:

Why To The Answer I Gave To The   I Am Starting To Feel _____
Prompt Above?

I Think Life Is: About _____.

WHAT I WANT OTHER KIDS TO KNOW....

MY THOUGHTS AND/OR MY DRAWINGS

OPENING MYSELF UP TO GREATNESS

Date: Mood:

Today I Felt: Today I Wanted To Know:

Today I Was Able To: Today I Am Thankful For:

Today I Enjoyed: What Bothered Me Today?

Today I Thought About: I Am Getting Better At:

Why To The Answer I Gave To The   I Am Starting To Feel _____
Prompt Above?

I Think Life Is: About _____.

OPENING MYSELF UP TO GREATNESS

Date: Mood:

Today I Felt: Today I Wanted To Know:

Today I Was Able To: Today I Am Thankful For:

Today I Enjoyed: What Bothered Me Today?

Today I Thought About: I Am Getting Better At:

Why To The Answer I Gave To The   I Am Starting To Feel _____
Prompt Above?

I Think Life Is: About _____.

I MAY NOT HAVE ALL THE ANSWERS, BUT I KNOW THAT GOD IS LOOKING OUT FOR ME.

OPENING MYSELF UP TO GREATNESS

Date: Mood:

Today I Felt: Today I Wanted To Know:

Today I Was Able To: Today I Am Thankful For:

Today I Enjoyed: What Bothered Me Today?

Today I Thought About: I Am Getting Better At:

Why To The Answer I Gave To The   I Am Starting To Feel _____
Prompt Above?

I Think Life Is: About _____.

OPENING MYSELF UP TO GREATNESS

Date: Mood:

Today I Felt: Today I Wanted To Know:

Today I Was Able To: Today I Am Thankful For:

Today I Enjoyed: What Bothered Me Today?

Today I Thought About: I Am Getting Better At:

Why To The Answer I Gave To The   I Am Starting To Feel _____
Prompt Above?

I Think Life Is: About _____.

MY THOUGHTS AND/OR MY DRAWINGS

OPENING MYSELF UP TO GREATNESS

Date: Mood:

Today I Felt: Today I Wanted To Know:

Today I Was Able To: Today I Am Thankful For:

Today I Enjoyed: What Bothered Me Today?

Today I Thought About: I Am Getting Better At:

Why To The Answer I Gave To The   I Am Starting To Feel _____
Prompt Above?

I Think Life Is: About _____.

OPENING MYSELF UP TO GREATNESS

Date: Mood:

Today I Felt: Today I Wanted To Know:

Today I Was Able To: Today I Am Thankful For:

Today I Enjoyed: What Bothered Me Today?

Today I Thought About: I Am Getting Better At:

Why To The Answer I Gave To The   I Am Starting To Feel _____
Prompt Above?

I Think Life Is: About _____.

WHAT I THINK ABOUT MY BIRTH PARENTS....

OPENING MYSELF UP TO GREATNESS

Date: Mood:

Today I Felt: Today I Wanted To Know:

Today I Was Able To: Today I Am Thankful For:

Today I Enjoyed: What Bothered Me Today?

Today I Thought About: I Am Getting Better At:

Why To The Answer I Gave To The   I Am Starting To Feel _____
Prompt Above?

I Think Life Is: About _____.

OPENING MYSELF UP TO GREATNESS

Date: Mood:

Today I Felt: Today I Wanted To Know:

Today I Was Able To: Today I Am Thankful For:

Today I Enjoyed: What Bothered Me Today?

Today I Thought About: I Am Getting Better At:

Why To The Answer I Gave To The   I Am Starting To Feel _____
Prompt Above?

I Think Life Is: About _____.

OPENING MYSELF UP TO GREATNESS

Date: Mood:

Today I Felt: Today I Wanted To Know:

Today I Was Able To: Today I Am Thankful For:

Today I Enjoyed: What Bothered Me Today?

Today I Thought About: I Am Getting Better At:

Why To The Answer I Gave To The   I Am Starting To Feel _____
Prompt Above?

I Think Life Is: About _____.

THINGS ARE GETTING BETTER.

OPENING MYSELF UP TO GREATNESS

Date: Mood:

Today I Felt: Today I Wanted To Know:

Today I Was Able To: Today I Am Thankful For:

Today I Enjoyed: What Bothered Me Today?

Today I Thought About: I Am Getting Better At:

Why To The Answer I Gave To The   I Am Starting To Feel _____
Prompt Above?

I Think Life Is: About _____.

OPENING MYSELF UP TO GREATNESS

Date: Mood:

Today I Felt: Today I Wanted To Know:

Today I Was Able To: Today I Am Thankful For:

Today I Enjoyed: What Bothered Me Today?

Today I Thought About: I Am Getting Better At:

Why To The Answer I Gave To The   I Am Starting To Feel _____
Prompt Above?

I Think Life Is: About _____.

I FEEL GOOD.

I HAVE A REASON TO FEEL GOOD.

THIS TIME IN MY LIFE IS ONLY TEMPORARY EVEN THOUGH IT FEELS SO LONG. I AM CHOOSING TO BE HAPPY.

OPENING MYSELF UP TO GREATNESS

Date: Mood:

Today I Felt: Today I Wanted To Know:

Today I Was Able To: Today I Am Thankful For:

Today I Enjoyed: What Bothered Me Today?

Today I Thought About: I Am Getting Better At:

Why To The Answer I Gave To The   I Am Starting To Feel _____
Prompt Above?

I Think Life Is: About _____.

OPENING MYSELF UP TO GREATNESS

Date: Mood:

Today I Felt: Today I Wanted To Know:

Today I Was Able To: Today I Am Thankful For:

Today I Enjoyed: What Bothered Me Today?

Today I Thought About: I Am Getting Better At:

Why To The Answer I Gave To The   I Am Starting To Feel _____
Prompt Above?

I Think Life Is: About _____.

OPENING MYSELF UP TO GREATNESS

Date: Mood:

Today I Felt: Today I Wanted To Know:

Today I Was Able To: Today I Am Thankful For:

Today I Enjoyed: What Bothered Me Today?

Today I Thought About: I Am Getting Better At:

Why To The Answer I Gave To The   I Am Starting To Feel _____
Prompt Above?

I Think Life Is: About _____.

MY THOUGHTS AND/OR MY DRAWINGS

I FEEL DIFFERENT FROM EVERYONE ELSE BECAUSE....

HOW DO I KNOW I FEEL DIFFERENT FROM EVERYONE ELSE?

OPENING MYSELF UP TO GREATNESS

Date: Mood:

Today I Felt: Today I Wanted To Know:

Today I Was Able To: Today I Am Thankful For:

Today I Enjoyed: What Bothered Me Today?

Today I Thought About: I Am Getting Better At:

Why To The Answer I Gave To The   I Am Starting To Feel _____
Prompt Above?

I Think Life Is: About _____.

OPENING MYSELF UP TO GREATNESS

Date: Mood:

Today I Felt: Today I Wanted To Know:

Today I Was Able To: Today I Am Thankful For:

Today I Enjoyed: What Bothered Me Today?

Today I Thought About: I Am Getting Better At:

Why To The Answer I Gave To The   I Am Starting To Feel _____
Prompt Above?

I Think Life Is: About _____.

I PRAY MY ANGER, DISAPPOINTMENT, AND LONELINESS GOES AWAY.

OPENING MYSELF UP TO GREATNESS

Date: Mood:

Today I Felt: Today I Wanted To Know:

Today I Was Able To: Today I Am Thankful For:

Today I Enjoyed: What Bothered Me Today?

Today I Thought About: I Am Getting Better At:

Why To The Answer I Gave To The   I Am Starting To Feel _____
Prompt Above?

I Think Life Is: About _____.

OPENING MYSELF UP TO GREATNESS

Date: Mood:

Today I Felt: Today I Wanted To Know:

Today I Was Able To: Today I Am Thankful For:

Today I Enjoyed: What Bothered Me Today?

Today I Thought About: I Am Getting Better At:

Why To The Answer I Gave To The   I Am Starting To Feel _____
Prompt Above?

I Think Life Is: About _____.

MY THOUGHTS AND/OR MY DRAWINGS

OPENING MYSELF UP TO GREATNESS

Date: Mood:

Today I Felt: Today I Wanted To Know:

Today I Was Able To: Today I Am Thankful For:

Today I Enjoyed: What Bothered Me Today?

Today I Thought About: I Am Getting Better At:

Why To The Answer I Gave To The   I Am Starting To Feel _____
Prompt Above?

I Think Life Is: About _____.

OPENING MYSELF UP TO GREATNESS

Date: Mood:

Today I Felt: Today I Wanted To Know:

Today I Was Able To: Today I Am Thankful For:

Today I Enjoyed: What Bothered Me Today?

Today I Thought About: I Am Getting Better At:

Why To The Answer I Gave To The   I Am Starting To Feel _____
Prompt Above?

I Think Life Is: About _____.

OPENING MYSELF UP TO GREATNESS

Date: Mood:

Today I Felt: Today I Wanted To Know:

Today I Was Able To: Today I Am Thankful For:

Today I Enjoyed: What Bothered Me Today?

Today I Thought About: I Am Getting Better At:

Why To The Answer I Gave To The   I Am Starting To Feel _____
Prompt Above?

I Think Life Is: About _____.

THEY MIGHT NOT BE MY REAL PARENTS, BUT I LOVE THEM LIKE THEY ARE.

I WILL LEARN TO LOVE AND BE LOVED.

OPENING MYSELF UP TO GREATNESS

Date: Mood:

Today I Felt: Today I Wanted To Know:

Today I Was Able To: Today I Am Thankful For:

Today I Enjoyed: What Bothered Me Today?

Today I Thought About: I Am Getting Better At:

Why To The Answer I Gave To The   I Am Starting To Feel _____
Prompt Above?

I Think Life Is: About _____.

OPENING MYSELF UP TO GREATNESS

Date: Mood:

Today I Felt: Today I Wanted To Know:

Today I Was Able To: Today I Am Thankful For:

Today I Enjoyed: What Bothered Me Today?

Today I Thought About: I Am Getting Better At:

Why To The Answer I Gave To The   I Am Starting To Feel _____
Prompt Above?

I Think Life Is: About _____.

MY THOUGHTS AND/OR MY DRAWINGS

OPENING MYSELF UP TO GREATNESS

Date: Mood:

Today I Felt: Today I Wanted To Know:

Today I Was Able To: Today I Am Thankful For:

Today I Enjoyed: What Bothered Me Today?

Today I Thought About: I Am Getting Better At:

Why To The Answer I Gave To The   I Am Starting To Feel _____
Prompt Above?

I Think Life Is: About _____.

OPENING MYSELF UP TO GREATNESS

Date: Mood:

Today I Felt: Today I Wanted To Know:

Today I Was Able To: Today I Am Thankful For:

Today I Enjoyed: What Bothered Me Today?

Today I Thought About: I Am Getting Better At:

Why To The Answer I Gave To The   I Am Starting To Feel _____
Prompt Above?

I Think Life Is: About _____.

5 THINGS NO ONE KNOWS ABOUT ME....

1.

2.

3.

4.

5.

MY THOUGHTS AND/OR MY DRAWINGS

OPENING MYSELF UP TO GREATNESS

Date: Mood:

Today I Felt: Today I Wanted To Know:

Today I Was Able To: Today I Am Thankful For:

Today I Enjoyed: What Bothered Me Today?

Today I Thought About: I Am Getting Better At:

Why To The Answer I Gave To The   I Am Starting To Feel _____
Prompt Above?

I Think Life Is: About _____.

OPENING MYSELF UP TO GREATNESS

Date: Mood:

Today I Felt: Today I Wanted To Know:

Today I Was Able To: Today I Am Thankful For:

Today I Enjoyed: What Bothered Me Today?

Today I Thought About: I Am Getting Better At:

Why To The Answer I Gave To The   I Am Starting To Feel _____
Prompt Above?

I Think Life Is: About _____.

SAY HI TO THE KID THAT IS READY TO CHANGE THE WORLD.

OPENING MYSELF UP TO GREATNESS

Date: Mood:

Today I Felt: Today I Wanted To Know:

Today I Was Able To: Today I Am Thankful For:

Today I Enjoyed: What Bothered Me Today?

Today I Thought About: I Am Getting Better At:

Why To The Answer I Gave To The   I Am Starting To Feel _____
Prompt Above?

I Think Life Is: About _____.

WHO AM I?

MY THOUGHTS AND/OR MY DRAWINGS

OPENING MYSELF UP TO GREATNESS

Date: Mood:

Today I Felt: Today I Wanted To Know:

Today I Was Able To: Today I Am Thankful For:

Today I Enjoyed: What Bothered Me Today?

Today I Thought About: I Am Getting Better At:

Why To The Answer I Gave To The   I Am Starting To Feel _____
Prompt Above?

I Think Life Is: About _____.

OPENING MYSELF UP TO GREATNESS

Date: Mood:

Today I Felt: Today I Wanted To Know:

Today I Was Able To: Today I Am Thankful For:

Today I Enjoyed: What Bothered Me Today?

Today I Thought About: I Am Getting Better At:

Why To The Answer I Gave To The   I Am Starting To Feel _____
Prompt Above?

I Think Life Is: About _____.

OPENING MYSELF UP TO GREATNESS

Date: Mood:

Today I Felt: Today I Wanted To Know:

Today I Was Able To: Today I Am Thankful For:

Today I Enjoyed: What Bothered Me Today?

Today I Thought About: I Am Getting Better At:

Why To The Answer I Gave To The   I Am Starting To Feel _____
Prompt Above?

I Think Life Is: About _____.

I AM RISING AND REALIZING AT THE SAME TIME.

I STOP BLAMING MY BIOLOGICAL PARENTS.

OPENING MYSELF UP TO GREATNESS

Date: Mood:

Today I Felt: Today I Wanted To Know.

Today I Was Able To: Today I Am Thankful For:

Today I Enjoyed: What Bothered Me Today?

Today I Thought About: I Am Getting Better At:

Why To The Answer I Gave To The   I Am Starting To Feel _____
Prompt Above?

I Think Life Is: About _____.

OPENING MYSELF UP TO GREATNESS

Date: Mood:

Today I Felt: Today I Wanted To Know:

Today I Was Able To: Today I Am Thankful For:

Today I Enjoyed: What Bothered Me Today?

Today I Thought About: I Am Getting Better At:

Why To The Answer I Gave To The   I Am Starting To Feel _____
Prompt Above?

I Think Life Is: About _____.

10 FIRST TIMES (WRITE TEN OF YOUR POSITIVE FIRST TIME EXPERIENCES)....

1.

2.

3.

4.

5.

6.

7.

8.

9.

10.

OPENING MYSELF UP TO GREATNESS

Date: Mood:

Today I Felt: Today I Wanted To Know:

Today I Was Able To: Today I Am Thankful For:

Today I Enjoyed: What Bothered Me Today?

Today I Thought About: I Am Getting Better At:

Why To The Answer I Gave To The   I Am Starting To Feel _____
Prompt Above?

I Think Life Is: About _____.

OPENING MYSELF UP TO GREATNESS

Date: Mood:

Today I Felt: Today I Wanted To Know:

Today I Was Able To: Today I Am Thankful For:

Today I Enjoyed: What Bothered Me Today?

Today I Thought About: I Am Getting Better At:

Why To The Answer I Gave To The   I Am Starting To Feel _____
Prompt Above?

I Think Life Is: About _____.

MY THOUGHTS AND/OR MY DRAWINGS

I HAVE A PROBLEM WITH....

OPENING MYSELF UP TO GREATNESS

Date: Mood:

Today I Felt: Today I Wanted To Know:

Today I Was Able To: Today I Am Thankful For:

Today I Enjoyed: What Bothered Me Today?

Today I Thought About: I Am Getting Better At:

Why To The Answer I Gave To The   I Am Starting To Feel _____
Prompt Above?

I Think Life Is: About _____.

OPENING MYSELF UP TO GREATNESS

Date: Mood:

Today I Felt: Today I Wanted To Know.

Today I Was Able To: Today I Am Thankful For:

Today I Enjoyed: What Bothered Me Today?

Today I Thought About: I Am Getting Better At:

Why To The Answer I Gave To The   I Am Starting To Feel _____
Prompt Above?

I Think Life Is: About _____.

OPENING MYSELF UP TO GREATNESS

Date: Mood:

Today I Felt: Today I Wanted To Know:

Today I Was Able To: Today I Am Thankful For:

Today I Enjoyed: What Bothered Me Today?

Today I Thought About: I Am Getting Better At:

Why To The Answer I Gave To The   I Am Starting To Feel _____
Prompt Above?

I Think Life Is: About _____.

I WILL SHATTER ALL OF YOUR MISCONCEPTION.

MY CONFUSION IS TEMPORARY, MY BLESSINGS ARE PERMANENT.

OPENING MYSELF UP TO GREATNESS

Date: Mood:

Today I Felt: Today I Wanted To Know:

Today I Was Able To: Today I Am Thankful For:

Today I Enjoyed: What Bothered Me Today?

Today I Thought About: I Am Getting Better At:

Why To The Answer I Gave To The   I Am Starting To Feel _____
Prompt Above?

I Think Life Is: About _____.

OPENING MYSELF UP TO GREATNESS

Date: Mood:

Today I Felt: Today I Wanted To Know:

Today I Was Able To: Today I Am Thankful For:

Today I Enjoyed: What Bothered Me Today?

Today I Thought About: I Am Getting Better At:

Why To The Answer I Gave To The   I Am Starting To Feel _____
Prompt Above?

I Think Life Is: About _____.

FOR MY BIRTHDAY, I WANT....

OPENING MYSELF UP TO GREATNESS

Date: Mood:

Today I Felt: Today I Wanted To Know:

Today I Was Able To: Today I Am Thankful For:

Today I Enjoyed: What Bothered Me Today?

Today I Thought About: I Am Getting Better At:

Why To The Answer I Gave To The   I Am Starting To Feel _____
Prompt Above?

I Think Life Is: About _____.

OPENING MYSELF UP TO GREATNESS

Date: Mood:

Today I Felt: Today I Wanted To Know:

Today I Was Able To: Today I Am Thankful For:

Today I Enjoyed: What Bothered Me Today?

Today I Thought About: I Am Getting Better At:

Why To The Answer I Gave To The   I Am Starting To Feel _____
Prompt Above?

I Think Life Is: About _____.

QUESTIONS I HAVE FOR MY ADOPTIVE PARENTS....

MY THOUGHTS AND/OR MY DRAWINGS

OPENING MYSELF UP TO GREATNESS

Date: Mood:

Today I Felt: Today I Wanted To Know:

Today I Was Able To: Today I Am Thankful For:

Today I Enjoyed: What Bothered Me Today?

Today I Thought About: I Am Getting Better At:

Why To The Answer I Gave To The   I Am Starting To Feel _____
Prompt Above?

I Think Life Is: About _____.

OPENING MYSELF UP TO GREATNESS

Date: Mood:

Today I Felt: Today I Wanted To Know:

Today I Was Able To: Today I Am Thankful For:

Today I Enjoyed: What Bothered Me Today?

Today I Thought About: I Am Getting Better At:

Why To The Answer I Gave To The   I Am Starting To Feel _____
Prompt Above?

I Think Life Is: About _____.

OPENING MYSELF UP TO GREATNESS

Date: Mood:

Today I Felt: Today I Wanted To Know:

Today I Was Able To: Today I Am Thankful For:

Today I Enjoyed: What Bothered Me Today?

Today I Thought About: I Am Getting Better At:

Why To The Answer I Gave To The   I Am Starting To Feel _____
Prompt Above?

I Think Life Is: About _____.

I INHALE POSITIVE THOUGHTS AND EXHALE NEGATIVE THOUGHTS.

I LOVE WHO I AM BECOMING.

OPENING MYSELF UP TO GREATNESS

Date: Mood:

Today I Felt: Today I Wanted To Know:

Today I Was Able To: Today I Am Thankful For:

Today I Enjoyed: What Bothered Me Today?

Today I Thought About: I Am Getting Better At:

Why To The Answer I Gave To The   I Am Starting To Feel _____
Prompt Above?

I Think Life Is: About _____.

OPENING MYSELF UP TO GREATNESS

Date: Mood:

Today I Felt: Today I Wanted To Know:

Today I Was Able To: Today I Am Thankful For:

Today I Enjoyed: What Bothered Me Today?

Today I Thought About: I Am Getting Better At:

Why To The Answer I Gave To The   I Am Starting To Feel _____
Prompt Above?

I Think Life Is: About _____.

MY THOUGHTS AND/OR MY DRAWINGS

OPENING MYSELF UP TO GREATNESS

Date: Mood:

Today I Felt: Today I Wanted To Know:

Today I Was Able To: Today I Am Thankful For:

Today I Enjoyed: What Bothered Me Today?

Today I Thought About: I Am Getting Better At:

Why To The Answer I Gave To The   I Am Starting To Feel _____
Prompt Above?

I Think Life Is: About _____.

I CAN'T TURN MY BACK ON MY ADOPTIVE PARENTS BECAUSE THEY WOULDN'T TURN THEIR BACK ON ME.

I AM LEARNING TO TRUST MY NEW FAMILY.

OPENING MYSELF UP TO GREATNESS

Date: Mood:

Today I Felt: Today I Wanted To Know:

Today I Was Able To: Today I Am Thankful For:

Today I Enjoyed: What Bothered Me Today?

Today I Thought About: I Am Getting Better At:

Why To The Answer I Gave To The   I Am Starting To Feel _____
Prompt Above?

I Think Life Is: About _____.

OPENING MYSELF UP TO GREATNESS

Date: Mood:

Today I Felt: Today I Wanted To Know:

Today I Was Able To: Today I Am Thankful For:

Today I Enjoyed: What Bothered Me Today?

Today I Thought About: I Am Getting Better At:

Why To The Answer I Gave To The   I Am Starting To Feel _____
Prompt Above?

I Think Life Is: About _____.

OPENING MYSELF UP TO GREATNESS

Date: Mood:

Today I Felt: Today I Wanted To Know.

Today I Was Able To: Today I Am Thankful For:

Today I Enjoyed: What Bothered Me Today?

Today I Thought About: I Am Getting Better At:

Why To The Answer I Gave To The   I Am Starting To Feel _____
Prompt Above?

I Think Life Is: About _____.

I WISH....

MY THOUGHTS AND/OR MY DRAWINGS

OPENING MYSELF UP TO GREATNESS

Date: Mood:

Today I Felt: Today I Wanted To Know:

Today I Was Able To: Today I Am Thankful For:

Today I Enjoyed: What Bothered Me Today?

Today I Thought About: I Am Getting Better At:

Why To The Answer I Gave To The   I Am Starting To Feel _____
Prompt Above?

I Think Life Is: About _____.

OPENING MYSELF UP TO GREATNESS

Date: Mood:

Today I Felt: Today I Wanted To Know:

Today I Was Able To: Today I Am Thankful For:

Today I Enjoyed: What Bothered Me Today?

Today I Thought About: I Am Getting Better At:

Why To The Answer I Gave To The   I Am Starting To Feel _____
Prompt Above?

I Think Life Is: About _____.

WHAT I REALLY WANT....

OPENING MYSELF UP TO GREATNESS

Date: Mood:

Today I Felt: Today I Wanted To Know:

Today I Was Able To: Today I Am Thankful For:

Today I Enjoyed: What Bothered Me Today?

Today I Thought About: I Am Getting Better At:

Why To The Answer I Gave To The   I Am Starting To Feel _____
Prompt Above?

I Think Life Is: About _____.

OPENING MYSELF UP TO GREATNESS

Date: Mood:

Today I Felt: Today I Wanted To Know:

Today I Was Able To: Today I Am Thankful For:

Today I Enjoyed: What Bothered Me Today?

Today I Thought About: I Am Getting Better At:

Why To The Answer I Gave To The   I Am Starting To Feel _____
Prompt Above?

I Think Life Is: About _____.

MY PAIN HAS TURNED INTO JOY.

OPENING MYSELF UP TO GREATNESS

Date: Mood:

Today I Felt: Today I Wanted To Know:

Today I Was Able To: Today I Am Thankful For:

Today I Enjoyed: What Bothered Me Today?

Today I Thought About: I Am Getting Better At:

Why To The Answer I Gave To The   I Am Starting To Feel _____
Prompt Above?

I Think Life Is: About _____.

OPENING MYSELF UP TO GREATNESS

Date: Mood:

Today I Felt: Today I Wanted To Know:

Today I Was Able To: Today I Am Thankful For:

Today I Enjoyed: What Bothered Me Today?

Today I Thought About: I Am Getting Better At:

Why To The Answer I Gave To The   I Am Starting To Feel _____
Prompt Above?

I Think Life Is: About _____.

OPENING MYSELF UP TO GREATNESS

Date: Mood:

Today I Felt: Today I Wanted To Know:

Today I Was Able To: Today I Am Thankful For:

Today I Enjoyed: What Bothered Me Today?

Today I Thought About: I Am Getting Better At:

Why To The Answer I Gave To The   I Am Starting To Feel _____
Prompt Above?

I Think Life Is: About _____.

DON'T BE MAD AT ME BECAUSE I HAVE GREAT PARENTS.

I DON'T HAVE TO WONDER IF GOD LOVES ME BECAUSE I KNOW.

OPENING MYSELF UP TO GREATNESS

Date: Mood:

Today I Felt: Today I Wanted To Know:

Today I Was Able To: Today I Am Thankful For:

Today I Enjoyed: What Bothered Me Today?

Today I Thought About: I Am Getting Better At:

Why To The Answer I Gave To The   I Am Starting To Feel _____
Prompt Above?

I Think Life Is: About _____.

OPENING MYSELF UP TO GREATNESS

Date: Mood:

Today I Felt: Today I Wanted To Know:

Today I Was Able To: Today I Am Thankful For:

Today I Enjoyed: What Bothered Me Today?

Today I Thought About: I Am Getting Better At:

Why To The Answer I Gave To The   I Am Starting To Feel _____
Prompt Above?

I Think Life Is: About _____.

OPENING MYSELF UP TO GREATNESS

Date: Mood:

Today I Felt: Today I Wanted To Know:

Today I Was Able To: Today I Am Thankful For:

Today I Enjoyed: What Bothered Me Today?

Today I Thought About: I Am Getting Better At:

Why To The Answer I Gave To The   I Am Starting To Feel _____
Prompt Above?

I Think Life Is: About _____.

I LISTEN TO MY PARENTS BECAUSE THEY KNOW WHAT'S BEST FOR ME.

I WAS BORN TO....

OPENING MYSELF UP TO GREATNESS

Date: Mood:

Today I Felt: Today I Wanted To Know:

Today I Was Able To: Today I Am Thankful For:

Today I Enjoyed: What Bothered Me Today?

Today I Thought About: I Am Getting Better At:

Why To The Answer I Gave To The Prompt Above?   I Am Starting To Feel _____

I Think Life Is: About _____.

OPENING MYSELF UP TO GREATNESS

Date: Mood:

Today I Felt: Today I Wanted To Know:

Today I Was Able To: Today I Am Thankful For:

Today I Enjoyed: What Bothered Me Today?

Today I Thought About: I Am Getting Better At:

Why To The Answer I Gave To The   I Am Starting To Feel _____
Prompt Above?

I Think Life Is: About _____.

WHO I AM WHEN I CAME HERE IS NOT WHO I WILL BE WHEN I LEAVE THIS HOME.

60218861R00150

Made in the USA
Columbia, SC
16 June 2019